The Outdoor Art Room
Autumn

Rita Storey

W
FRANKLIN WATTS
LONDON • SYDNEY

Franklin Watts
First published in Great Britain in 2015 by The Watts Publishing Group

Series editor: Sarah Peutrill
Art direction: Peter Scoulding
Series designed and created for Franklin Watts by Storeybooks
rita@storeybooks.co.uk
Designer: Rita Storey
Editor: Sarah Ridley
Photography: Tudor Photography, Banbury
Cover images: Tudor Photography, Banbury
Cover design: Cathryn Gilbert

Every attempt has been made to clear copyright. Should there be any
inadvertent omission please apply to the publisher for rectification.

Dewey number 745.5
HB ISBN 978 1 4451 3967 8
Library ebook ISBN 978 1 4451 3968 5

A CIP catalogue record for this book is available
from the British Library.

Printed in China

MIX
Paper from
responsible sources
FSC® C104740
FSC
www.fsc.org

Franklin Watts
An imprint of
Hachette Children's Group
Part of The Watts Publishing Group
Carmelite House
50 Victoria Embankment
London EC4Y 0DZ

An Hachette UK Company
www.hachette.co.uk

www.franklinwatts.co.uk

Before you start

Some of the projects in this book require scissors, sharp tools or
plaster of Paris. When using these things we would recommend that
children are supervised by a responsible adult.

Contents

All about autumn

Autumn is a great time to get outside before the start of winter, when the days grow shorter and the weather becomes colder. This book is full of art projects and fun things to collect, make and do outside in autumn using, amongst other things, fruits, pine cones, leaves and seeds. Have fun!

When is autumn?

Autumn occurs at different times of the year in different parts of the world. In the northern half of the world, autumn lasts from September to November. In the southern half, it lasts from March to May. During the autumn months, the days get shorter and the nights are longer.

Autumn is the season between summer and winter. In some parts of the world it is called 'fall' because in autumn the leaves fall off the trees. There is often mist early in the mornings, and sometimes fog. The temperature grows colder and there may be frosts.

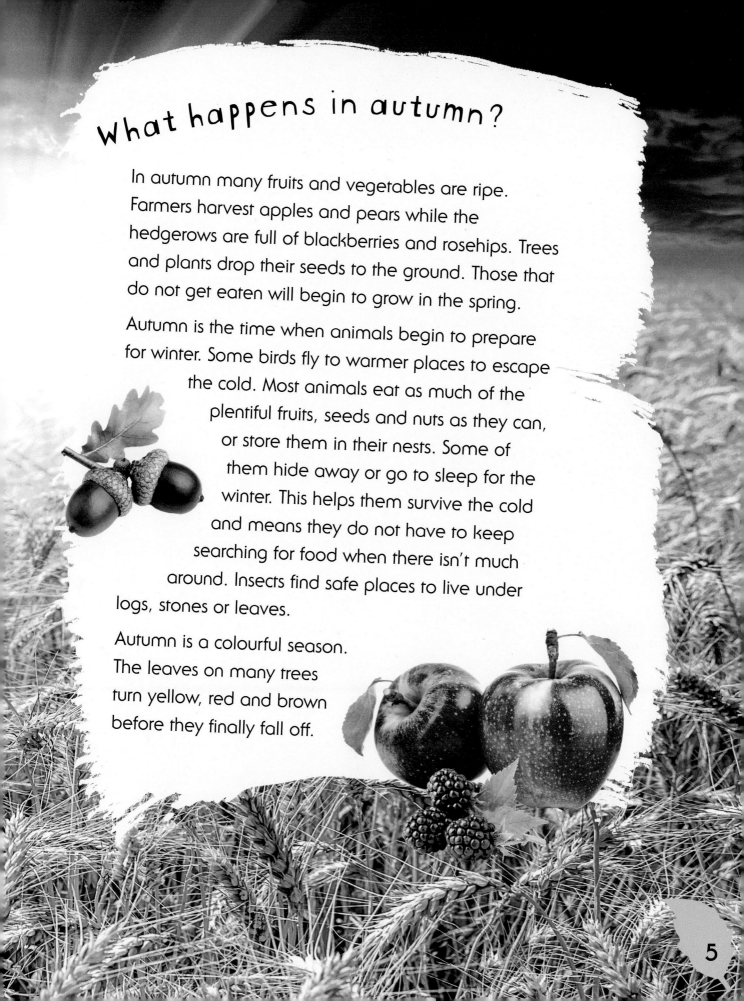

What happens in autumn?

In autumn many fruits and vegetables are ripe. Farmers harvest apples and pears while the hedgerows are full of blackberries and rosehips. Trees and plants drop their seeds to the ground. Those that do not get eaten will begin to grow in the spring.

Autumn is the time when animals begin to prepare for winter. Some birds fly to warmer places to escape the cold. Most animals eat as much of the plentiful fruits, seeds and nuts as they can, or store them in their nests. Some of them hide away or go to sleep for the winter. This helps them survive the cold and means they do not have to keep searching for food when there isn't much around. Insects find safe places to live under logs, stones or leaves.

Autumn is a colourful season. The leaves on many trees turn yellow, red and brown before they finally fall off.

A bug hotel

The bugs in your garden need to find somewhere safe and warm in the autumn where they can spend the winter. Help them by building this smart bug hotel.

You will need:

* wooden seed tray

* scissors

* 4 cardboard juice cartons

* glue and spreader

* hollow plant stems (ask an adult to find these for you in the garden)

* moss or grass * pine cones

* raffia or string

* dry leaves

The leaves and moss in the bug hotel provide food for the minibeasts as well as a sheltered spot to survive the colder weather.

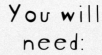 Ask an adult to cut the juice cartons into sections that are the same depth as the seed tray.

2 Glue the sections into the box as shown in the picture above.

3 Fill three of the sections with lengths of hollow plant stems cut to the depth of the box.

4 Fill two of the sections with moss or grass. Pack pine cones into two more sections.

Bugs in autumn and winter

Bugs (minibeasts) all have their own way of surviving through winter. Some of them turn into a pupa (a soft grub with a hard casing) in autumn, and wait until winter is over. Others, including slugs, snails, millipedes, ladybirds and woodlice, find a dark, sheltered place to hide from the cold.

5 Fill two sections with raffia or string.

6 Pack leaves into the spaces between all the sections. Turn the box upright. Place it outside where it is dark, dry and sheltered, such as under a hedge or bush. Wait for the first visitors to move in.

7

Sparkly leaf garland

On frosty, autumn days the colourful leaves sparkle with tiny crystals of ice. Make some leaves glitter like frost in this twinkly leaf garland.

You will need:

* autumn leaves
* PVA glue
* paintbrush
* plate * glitter
* small pegs and a length of string
* 1m of yellow raffia
* measuring tape
* stapler

1 Collect a pile of colourful autumn leaves.

2 Paint the leaves with PVA glue and leave them to dry. Turn the leaves over and repeat. This will help the leaves to last longer without drying out.

Leaves

Deciduous trees lose all their leaves in winter. Evergreen trees have thick, tough leaves which stay green and alive all winter. They lose their leaves gradually throughout the year and grow new replacements.

3 Paint PVA glue around the edge of each leaf.

4 Place the leaf on a plate and sprinkle with glitter.

5 Shake off the surplus glitter onto the plate. Tie the piece of string between two points and use a peg to hang the leaf up to dry. Repeat steps 1–5 with more leaves.

6 Staple the stem of a leaf 20cm from the end of the raffia. Overlap another leaf and staple it on. Continue to staple on more leaves until you are 20cm from the other end of the raffia. Find a good spot to hang up your sparkly leaf garland.

Leaf bird tree

Birds are easy to see in autumn as they are busy collecting seeds and berries. You can collect fallen leaves and broken twigs to make these exotic birds.

You will need:

* twig (measuring 30cm in length)
* green paint
* paintbrush
* glue and spreader
* small black beads
* medium-sized oval-shaped leaves
* small oval-shaped leaves
* feathery-shaped leaves

Migration

Some birds fly to a warmer country when the weather turns colder in the autumn, and return the following spring. This is called migration.

1 Paint the twig green. Leave it to dry.

2 Glue a small black bead onto the front of a medium-sized leaf.

3 Glue a small leaf onto the medium-sized leaf, as shown in the picture.

10

4 Glue on a leaf that looks like a feathery tail.

5 Repeat steps 1–4 to make more birds.

6 Put a blob of glue onto the back of each leaf bird. Glue them onto the twig and leave them to dry.

7 Display your model in an empty bottle indoors or push the end of the twig into the ground outside.

Pine cone lion

Turn a pine cone into a friendly yellow lion. Can you think of any other creatures that you could make using a pine cone?

(A) Ball of clay, flattened into a circle measuring 3cm across

(B) Thick 'sausage' of clay, 4cm long

(C) 2 x 'sausages' of clay, 2cm long

(D) 2 x balls of clay, flattened into circles measuring 2cm across

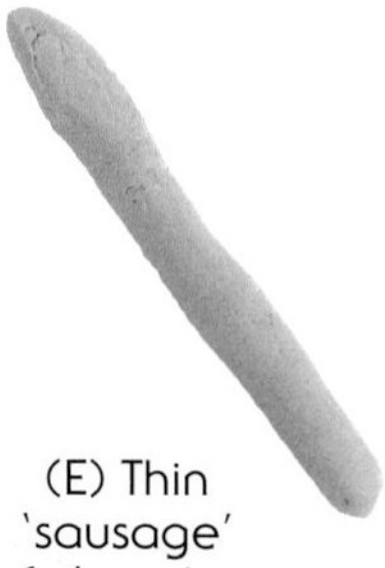

(E) Thin 'sausage' of clay, 4cm long

You will need:

* air-dry clay
* ruler
* pine cone
* paintbrush
* yellow paint
* brown felt-tip pen

1 Make the shapes shown in the picture above out of air-dry clay.

Pine cones

Pine cones contain the seeds of pine trees. The scales of a pine cone open when it is wet and close when it is dry. A lot of pine cones fall off the trees in autumn.

2 Press the circle of clay (A) onto the pointed end of the cone.

3 Press the 'sausage' of clay (B) onto the other end of the cone.

4 Press the two small 'sausages' of clay (C) onto each side of the lion's body at the front.

5 Press the small flat circles of clay (D) onto each side of the lion's body. Press the thin 'sausage' of clay (E) onto the back of the lion's body. Leave to dry overnight.

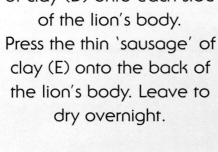
6 Paint the clay yellow. Leave to dry for 2–3 hours.

7 Finish the lion by drawing a friendly face with the felt-tip pen.

Autumn tracks

Be an animal tracker and see if you can find out what animals are using your garden from the tracks that they leave behind.

On a dry day put a layer of soft sand outside on a path. Leave the sand for a few hours or overnight. If you are lucky there may be animal tracks in it. If not press a small shoe into the sand and follow steps 2–6.

You will need:
* sand
* rubber gloves
* plaster of Paris
* plastic mixing bowl
* spoon
* paintbrush
* paint

Ask an adult to put on rubber gloves and follow the directions on the packet to mix the plaster of Paris into a thin paste.

Take care!
Ask an adult to help with this activity. Follow the instructions carefully and ask the adult to dispose of any extra plaster of Paris.

Spoon the mixture into the tracks or shoe print. Take care not to move the sand as you do so. Leave to set for at least 30 minutes.

Animal tracks

Here are some animal tracks:

Dog   Cat   Fox

 4 When the plaster of Paris is completely dry, lift it out of the sand. Wash it under a running tap.

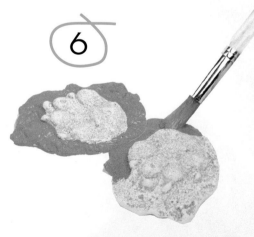

5 Put some sand in a plastic container. Press the footprint or track into the sand. Lift it out. Repeat steps 3–4 to make more plaster of Paris casts.

6 Paint the tracks and display them in the garden.

Watercolour leaves

Look closely at some autumn leaves. There are lots of different colours in each leaf. This way of painting uses watered down paint to make colours fade into each other, as they do on autumn leaves.

You will need:

* pencil
* different shaped leaves
* thick white paper or watercolour paper
* scissors
* water
* paintbrush
* red, yellow, green and brown watercolour paints
* jar of water to clean your brush
* sheet of A3 white paper
* glue and spreader

1 Use a pencil to draw around a leaf onto the thick white paper.

2 Cut out the leaf shape. Use a clean brush to paint the paper leaf with water.

3 Mix up some watery red paint and paint it onto part of the leaf. Let the colour spread. Leave to dry.

4 Mix up some watery yellow paint and paint it onto another part of the leaf. Let the colours spread. Leave to dry. Repeat with the pale green paint.

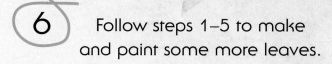

5 Using the pointed tip of the paintbrush handle, draw the veins of the leaf in red paint. Leave to dry.

6 Follow steps 1–5 to make and paint some more leaves.

7 Using brown paint, paint a bare tree on the large sheet of paper.

8 Glue the paper leaves onto your tree.

Autumn bowl

This leaf-shaped glittery bowl is perfect for displaying an autumn collection of pine cones and seed pods.

You will need:

* rolling pin
* air-dry clay
* large leaf
* kitchen knife
* small cereal bowl
* paintbrush
* red, yellow, orange and brown paint
* jar of water to clean your brush
* glue and spreader
* glitter
* seeds and pine cones

1 Roll out a circle of clay just larger than the leaf. Press the leaf onto the clay with the back of the leaf touching the clay.

2 Cut around the leaf with the kitchen knife. Remove the extra clay.

3 Carefully remove the leaf to reveal a clay leaf.

 4 Drape the clay leaf over the small bowl. Leave it to dry overnight.

5 Paint the inside of the bowl with autumn colours. Leave to dry.

 6 Turn the clay leaf over. Paint the back using red paint. Leave to dry.

7 Spread glue around the edge of the bowl. Sprinkle some glitter over the glue. Leave to dry. Fill the bowl with autumn seeds and pine cones.

Apple print wrapping

Make some cool wrapping paper and matching gift tags with windfall apples.

You will need:

* apple, cut in half from the stalk to the base
* red and green paint
* paintbrush
* jar of water to wash your brush
* 2 leaves from an apple tree

(for the wrapping paper)

* sheet of A3 white paper

(for the gift tag)

* piece of thin white card, 7cm x 7cm
* scissors
* hole punch
* green raffia

To make the paper

1 Paint the cut side of one of the apple halves with red paint.

2 Press the apple down on the A3 paper to make some red apple prints. Leave to dry.

3 Paint the other half of the apple with green paint. Make green apple prints on the paper. Leave to dry.

Harvest

Many fruits, vegetables and grains are ready to eat in autumn. We harvest these food crops by picking, collecting and storing them. When apples are ripe they fall or are blown off the tree if they are not picked. These apples are called windfalls.

4 Paint one leaf green. Press it down above each red apple to make leaf prints. Paint the other leaf red. Press it down above each green apple to make leaf prints.

To make the tag

Paint the cut side of the apple with red paint. Press it down, close to the bottom of the card to make an apple print.

1

2

3 Use scissors to cut around the apple print. Punch a hole in the top of the tag, as shown.

Paint the leaf green and use it to print two leaves at the top of the red apple. Leave to dry.

4 Thread the raffia through the hole in the tag. Wrap up a present in the apple print paper and use the raffia to tie on the tag.

Animal collage

Leaves can be all sorts of different shapes. Look at some leaves and think about what animals you could make with them.

You will need:

(for the caterpillar)

* green leaves
* sheet of A4 green paper
* glue and spreader
* 2 googly eyes

(for the hedgehog)

* leaf, painted brown
* spiky-shaped leaves
* sheet of A4 blue paper
* glue
* googly eye

1 Arrange the leaves in a wiggly line, as shown in the picture. Glue them onto the green paper.

2 To complete the caterpillar, glue on two googly eyes.

Hibernation

Some animals find a sheltered spot and go to sleep through the winter. This is called hibernation. Hedgehogs hibernate amongst piles of leaves.

1 Glue the brown painted leaf on the right-hand side of the blue paper with the point facing to the right.

2 Glue the spiky leaves onto the paper as shown in the finished picture. To complete the hedgehog, glue on a googly eye.

Seed picture

Pumpkins are often used to make lanterns for Halloween. You can also use the seeds to make a striking pumpkin picture. You could try growing a pumpkin in your garden.

1 Ask an adult to cut the top off the pumpkin. Scoop out the seeds into the bowl.

You will need:

* pumpkin
* knife for an adult to use
* spoon * bowl * plate
* orange food colouring
* white crayon
* sheet of A4 black card
* glue and paintbrush

2 Wash the seeds in water.

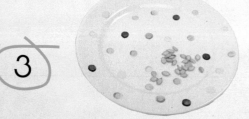

3 Spread them out on a plate to dry for a day.

Seeds

Many plants and trees produce fruit and seeds in the autumn. The seeds from one pumpkin could grow into lots more pumpkins next spring. Acorns are the seeds of oak trees. Squirrels bury acorns in holes in the ground to eat when food is scarce in winter.

4 Put the seeds into a bowl. Add a few drops of orange food colouring and stir until the seeds are orange.

5 Spread the orange seeds on a plate to dry.

6 Use a white crayon to draw the outline of a pumpkin on black card. Add eyes, a nose and a mouth. Paint over the outline with glue.

7 Stick seeds onto the lines of glue. You may need to apply more glue if this takes a long while.

8 Spread glue over the rest of the shape, except for the eyes, nose and mouth. Stick more seeds to your pumpkin picture to finish it.

Autumn masterpiece

C ollect leaves, berries, and seed pods that have fallen on the ground. Turn them into a work of art and frame them like a painting in an art gallery.

You will need:

* 2 x sheets of A3 card
* orange, red and yellow paint
* large paintbrush
* jar of water to wash your brush
* white glue in a bottle with a nozzle
* leaves, berries and seed pods
* gold paint
* scissors

Take care!
Some autumn berries are poisonous. Do not eat any berries unless you are certain what they are. Always wash your hands after picking berries.

1 Use the large paintbrush to paint the A3 card in bright patches of orange, red and yellow. Leave to dry.

2 Drizzle swirls of white glue all over the painting.

3 Stick the leaves, berries and seeds onto the swirls of glue. Leave to dry.

4 Ask an adult to cut the centre out of the second piece of A3 card to make a frame. Decorate the frame with swirls of white glue. Leave to dry. Paint the frame gold and leave it to dry.

5 Spread glue onto the back of the frame. Glue it onto the front of the picture.

Falling leaves

Bring the colours of the autumn inside with this pretty window decoration.

You will need:

* 1 metre length of contact paper (available from art and stationery shops)
* measuring tape
* a heavy object or paperweight
* autumn leaves
* sticky tape

Autumn leaves

Green pigments in leaves use sunlight, water and gases in the air to make food for the plant. When there is not much sunlight, the green pigments die off, revealing the yellow or red pigments that were there all along.

1 Place the contact paper on a flat surface. Use the measuring tape to measure out 1 metre and carefully peel off the top layer. Place a plant pot or other heavy object onto the end to stop it rolling back.

2 Arrange the leaves on the sticky surface of the contact paper.

3 Ask an adult to help you roll the top layer of sticky paper over the leaves. Press firmly in place.

4 Tape the falling leaf picture onto a window using sticky tape.

The leaves trapped inside the sticky contact paper will last for several days before they dry out and fade.

Autumn words

berry small juicy fruit without a stone

frost frozen dew or water vapour

Halloween festival celebrated on 31 October when children dress up in scary masks and costumes and carve pumpkins to make lanterns

harvest gathering in grain or other food crops

hibernation when animals go into a deep sleep to survive winter

insect a small animal that has three parts to its body, six legs and often has two pairs of wings

migration when animals or birds move from one area to another every year, according to the seasons

minibeast a small animal that has no backbone, such as a spider, slug or fly

pigment the natural colour occurring in plant or animal cells

pine cone woody fruit of a pine tree

pupa the stage of an insect's lifecycle between the young and the adult

rosehip red fruits of wild roses found in many hedgerows

seed pod a type of fruit which ripens and splits to reveal seeds

windfall an apple, pear or other fruit, blown down from a tree by the wind

Find out more

www.dltk-holidays.com/fall/
Lots of great autumn themed crafts and activities.

www.bbc.co.uk/nature/ collections/p00bdxqw
The BBC Nature video collection of short films about wildlife in autumn.

www.naturedetectives.org. uk/autumn/
Autumn ideas and activities from the Woodland Trust.

Note to parents and teachers: every effort has been made by the Publishers to ensure that these websites are suitable for children, that they are of the highest educational value, and that they contain no inappropriate or offensive material. However, because of the nature of the Internet, it is impossible to guarantee that the contents of these sites will not be altered. We strongly advise that Internet access is supervised by a responsible adult.

Index

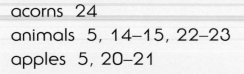